My Path to Math
1 2 3 4 5 6 7 8 9

CALENDAR MATH

Lisa Colozza Cocca

Crabtree Publishing Company

www.crabtreebooks.com

Author: Lisa Colozza Cocca

Publishing plan research and development:
Sean Charlebois, Reagan Miller
Crabtree Publishing Company

Editors: Reagan Miller, Crystal Sikkens, Ruth Frederick, Leslie Jenkins, Phyllis Jelinek

Proofreaders: Kelly McNiven, Lisa Slone

Editorial director: Kathy Middleton

Production coordinator: Shivi Sharma

Creative director: Amir Abbasi

Cover design: Margaret Amy Salter

Photo research: Nivisha Sinha, Crystal Sikkens

Production coordinator and prepress technician: Margaret Amy Salter

Print coordinators: Katherine Berti, Margaret Amy Salter

Photographs:

Cover: Thinkstock; Page 1: Thinkstock; Page 4: Sergio Stakhnyk / Shutterstock.com (t); Page 4: freesoulproduction / Shutterstock.com (b); Page 5: Gunnar Pippel / Shutterstock.com (t); Page 5: fotographic1980 / Shutterstock.com (b); Page 6: Tang Yan Song / Shutterstock.com (t); Page 6: ajfi / Shutterstock.com (b); Page 7: iaRada / Shutterstock.com (t); Page 7: Ivanova Kristina / Shutterstock.com (b); Page 10: 3445128471 / Shutterstock.com; Page 13: iaRada / Shutterstock.com (l); Page 13: iaRada / Shutterstock.com (r); Page 14: Togataki / Shutterstock.com; Page 15: Togataki / Shutterstock.com; Page 16: glossygirl21 / Shutterstock.com; Page 17: mattasbestos / Shutterstock.com; Page 18: shaileshnanal / Shutterstock.com; Page 19: iaRada / Shutterstock.com; Page 21: David Lee / Shutterstock.com.

Artwork Created by Planman technologies: 8; 9; 11; 12; 20; 21; 23.

(t = top, b = bottom, l = left, c= center, r = right)

Library and Archives Canada Cataloguing in Publication

Cocca, Lisa Colozza, 1957-
    Calendar math / Lisa Colozza Cocca.

(My path to math)
Includes index.
Issued in print and electronic formats.
ISBN 978-0-7787-1075-2 (bound).--ISBN 978-0-7787-1091-2 (pbk.).--
ISBN 978-1-4271-9272-1 (pdf).--ISBN 978-1-4271-9196-0 (html)

    1. Time measurements--Juvenile literature. 2. Calendar--Juvenile
literature. I. Title. II. Series: My path to math

QB209.5.C63 2013   j529'.7   C2013-902662-2
                                           C2013-902663-0

Library of Congress Cataloging-in-Publication Data

CIP available at Library of Congress

Crabtree Publishing Company

www.crabtreebooks.com   1-800-387-7650

Printed in the USA/052013/JA20130412

Published in Canada
Crabtree Publishing
616 Welland Ave.
St. Catharines, ON
L2M 5V6

Published in the United States
Crabtree Publishing
PMB 59051
350 Fifth Avenue, 59th Floor
New York, New York 10118

Published in the United Kingdom
Crabtree Publishing
Maritime House
Basin Road North, Hove
BN41 1WR

Published in Australia
Crabtree Publishing
3 Charles Street
Coburg North
VIC, 3058

Contents

What is a Calendar?

Haru is having a birthday party! Al and Leti are both excited to go. They want to know how to measure the amount of time until the **day** of Haru's party.

Al's mom tells them that there are different tools to measure different things. A thermometer is a tool. It measures temperature.

A ruler is a tool, too. A ruler shows how long something is.

A thermometer shows how hot or cold something is.

A ruler is a tool that measures length.

The children need a tool that measures time.

These tools measure time:

A **clock** measures time in seconds, minutes, and hours.

A **calendar** measures time in days, **weeks**, **months**, and **years**.

December						2013
Sun	Mon	Tue	Wed	Thu	Fri	Sat
1	2	3	4	5	6	7
8	9	10	11	12	13	14
15	16	17	18	19	20	21
22	23	24	25	26	27	28
29	30	31				

Activity Box

The party is in two weeks. What tool should Al and Leti use for measuring?

Kinds of Calendars

Al and Leti now know they will use a calendar to measure the time until the party. There are many kinds of calendars.

December

31

Some calendars show one day at a time.

Some calendars show one week at a time.

9 Sunday	10 Monday	11 Tuesday	12 Wednesday	13 Thursday	14 Friday	15 Saturday

Some calendars show
one month at a time.

May

Sun	Mon	Tue	Wed	Thu	Fri	Sat
			1	2	3	4
5	6	7	8	9	10	11
12	13	14	15	16	17	18
19	20	21	22	23	24	25
26	27	28	29	30	31	

Some calendars show
one year at a time.

2013

January
Sun	Mon	Tue	Wed	Thu	Fri	Sat
		1	2	3	4	5
6	7	8	9	10	11	12
13	14	15	16	17	18	19
20	21	22	23	24	25	26
27	28	29	30	31		

February
Sun	Mon	Tue	Wed	Thu	Fri	Sat
					1	2
3	4	5	6	7	8	9
10	11	12	13	14	15	16
17	18	19	20	21	22	23
24	25	26	27	28		

March
Sun	Mon	Tue	Wed	Thu	Fri	Sat
					1	2
3	4	5	6	7	8	9
10	11	12	13	14	15	16
17	18	19	20	21	22	23
24/31	25	26	27	28	29	30

April
Sun	Mon	Tue	Wed	Thu	Fri	Sat
	1	2	3	4	5	6
7	8	9	10	11	12	13
14	15	16	17	18	19	20
21	22	23	24	25	26	27
28	29	30				

May
Sun	Mon	Tue	Wed	Thu	Fri	Sat
			1	2	3	4
5	6	7	8	9	10	11
12	13	14	15	16	17	18
19	20	21	22	23	24	25
26	27	28	29	30	31	

June
Sun	Mon	Tue	Wed	Thu	Fri	Sat
						1
2	3	4	5	6	7	8
9	10	11	12	13	14	15
16	17	18	19	20	21	22
23/30	24	25	26	27	28	29

July
Sun	Mon	Tue	Wed	Thu	Fri	Sat
	1	2	3	4	5	6
7	8	9	10	11	12	13
14	15	16	17	18	19	20
21	22	23	24	25	26	27
28	29	30	31			

August
Sun	Mon	Tue	Wed	Thu	Fri	Sat
				1	2	3
4	5	6	7	8	9	10
11	12	13	14	15	16	17
18	19	20	21	22	23	24
25	26	27	28	29	30	31

September
Sun	Mon	Tue	Wed	Thu	Fri	Sat
1	2	3	4	5	6	7
8	9	10	11	12	13	14
15	16	17	18	19	20	21
22	23	24	25	26	27	28
29	30					

October
Sun	Mon	Tue	Wed	Thu	Fri	Sat
		1	2	3	4	5
6	7	8	9	10	11	12
13	14	15	16	17	18	19
20	21	22	23	24	25	26
27	28	29	30	31		

November
Sun	Mon	Tue	Wed	Thu	Fri	Sat
					1	2
3	4	5	6	7	8	9
10	11	12	13	14	15	16
17	18	19	20	21	22	23
24	25	26	27	28	29	30

December
Sun	Mon	Tue	Wed	Thu	Fri	Sat
1	2	3	4	5	6	7
8	9	10	11	12	13	14
15	16	17	18	19	20	21
22	23	24	25	26	27	28
29	30	31				

Parts of a Calendar

Al and Leti pick a calendar that shows one month at a time. Each day in a month has a number. Each new month starts with the number 1. The day's number, month, and year is the **date**. Al points at the last number. It shows how many days are in the month.

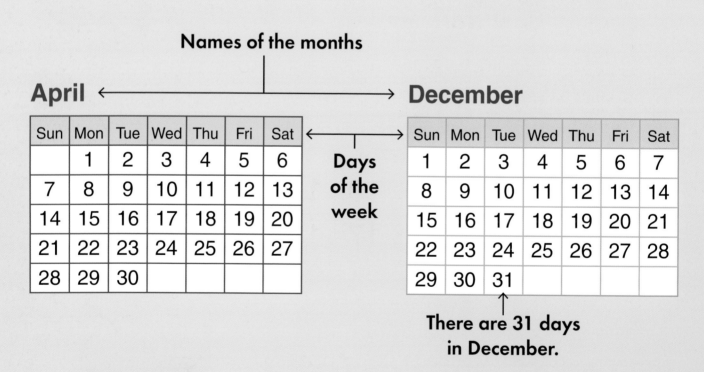

Names of the months

April ← → **December**

Days of the week

Sun	Mon	Tue	Wed	Thu	Fri	Sat
	1	2	3	4	5	6
7	8	9	10	11	12	13
14	15	16	17	18	19	20
21	22	23	24	25	26	27
28	29	30				

Sun	Mon	Tue	Wed	Thu	Fri	Sat
1	2	3	4	5	6	7
8	9	10	11	12	13	14
15	16	17	18	19	20	21
22	23	24	25	26	27	28
29	30	31				

There are 31 days in December.

Activity Box

Look at the two calendars above.
Which month has more days?

The calendar has rows and columns.

Rows go side to side.

Columns go up and down.

Leti sees a row. She reads it like a page in a book. She reads from left to right. The top row of the calendar shows the days of the week.

Al finds Sunday in the top row. He slides his finger down the column from top to bottom. Each day in this column is on Sunday.

Column
↓

December

Sun	Mon	Tue	Wed	Thu	Fri	Sat
1	2	3	4	5	6	7
8	9	10	11	12	13	14
15	16	17	18	19	20	21
22	23	24	25	26	27	28
29	30	31				

Row →

Activity Box

Look at the December calendar above.
Are there more days on Monday or Saturday?

Repeating Days and Months

Al sees that there are seven days in one week. Sunday is the first day of the week. Saturday is the last day of the week. Al's mom tells him that after Saturday a new week starts again on Sunday. Al's mom asks him to write the days of the week in order.

Al writes:

Sunday → Monday → Tuesday → Wednesday

Thursday → Friday → Saturday

Activity Box

What day comes after Monday?
What day comes before Saturday?

Leti looks at the calendar and sees there are 12 months in a year. She says the months in order. Leti finds last year's calendar. It has the same 12 months.

Al's mom tells them that the days of the week and the months of the year always repeat in the same pattern. A **pattern** is something that repeats over and over again.

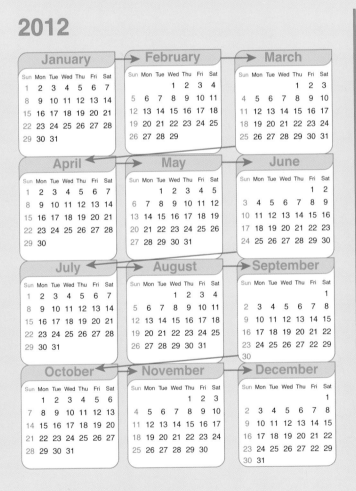

2012

2013

Activity Box

Which month comes after October?
Which month comes before June?

Days in a Month

Al and Leti look at the 12 months of the year. They see that some months have more days than others. Al's mom teaches them a poem to remember how many days are in each month.

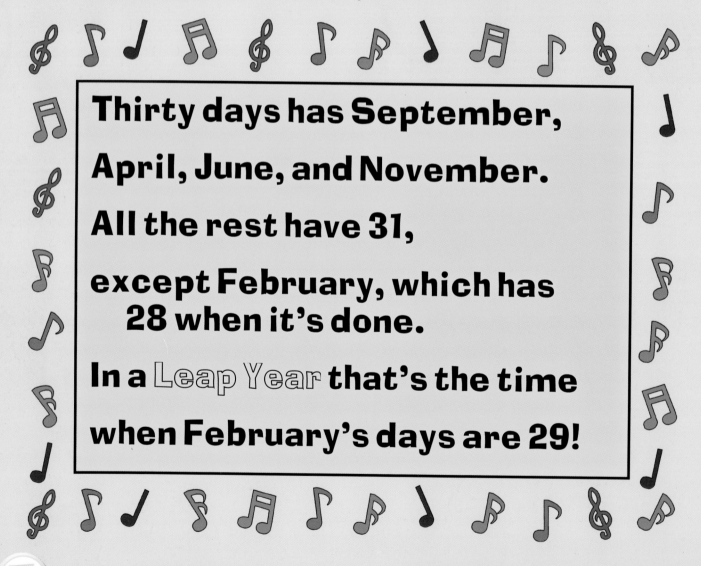

Thirty days has September,

April, June, and November.

All the rest have 31,

except February, which has 28 when it's done.

In a Leap Year that's the time

when February's days are 29!

Al and Leti also notice that not every month starts on the same day of the week. If a month ends on a Wednesday, the first day of the next month will be a Thursday.

The first day of June is on Saturday.

May

Sun	Mon	Tue	Wed	Thu	Fri	Sat
			1	2	3	4
5	6	7	8	9	10	11
12	13	14	15	16	17	18
19	20	21	22	23	24	25
26	27	28	29	30	31	

June

Sun	Mon	Tue	Wed	Thu	Fri	Sat
						1
2	3	4	5	6	7	8
9	10	11	12	13	14	15
16	17	18	19	20	21	22
23/30	24	25	26	27	28	29

The last day of May is on Friday.

Activity Box

If September ends on a Monday, on which day of the week will October begin?

Calendar Patterns

Leti looks at the calendar. She also sees patterns in the numbers.

November

Sun	Mon	Tue	Wed	Thu	Fri	Sat
					1	2
3	4	5	6	7	8	9
10	11	12	13	14	15	16
17	18	19	20	21	22	23
24	25	26	27	28	29	30

Leti notices that each day on the calendar is one number larger than the day before it. To find out the next day's number, she adds 1 to the day before it.

1+1=2

2+1=3

3+1=4

Al looks at the columns in the calendar. He reads from top to bottom and sees another pattern. Each number is 7 more than the number above it.

$2+7=9$

$9+7=16$

$16+7=23$

$23+7= ?$

Can you fill in the next answer?
Use the calendar on page 14 to help you.

Activity Box

Using both Leti and Al's patterns, fill in the missing numbers on this September calendar. Hint: Use the poem on page 12 to find out how many days are in September.

September

Sun	Mon	Tue	Wed	Thu	Fri	Sat
1	2	3	4	5	6	7
8	9	10			13	14
15	16	17	18	19	20	
	23	24	25	26	27	28

Counting Time

Today is Sunday, May 5. Al sees that Haru's birthday party is on Sunday, May 19. Al wants to know how many days until the party. Al puts his finger on today's date. He counts the days between today's date and the party day. The party is 14 days away.

HAPPY BIRTHDAY

You are invited to my birthday party on May 19. It will be lots of fun!

Leti wants to know how many weeks that is. She starts counting on May 5. Each time she moves down a row it is one week. The party is two weeks away.

May

Sun	Mon	Tue	Wed	Thu	Fri	Sat
			1	2	3	4
(5)	6	7	8	9	10	11
12	13	14	15	16	17	18
(19)	20	21	22	23	24	25
26	27	28	29	30	31	

Activity Box

You can also count time using months. If today's date is January 6, one month from today would be February 6. How many months away would April 6 be?

Hint: You can use the calendars on page 11 to help you.

Yesterday, Today, and Tomorrow

It is time for Leti to leave Al's house. Leti has to go to school tomorrow. She knows that tomorrow is one day after today. Today's date is Sunday, May 5. She uses a calendar to find tomorrow's date. Leti looks at the day to the right. Tomorrow will be Monday, May 6.

Al was at Leti's house yesterday. Yesterday is the day before today. Al puts his finger on today's date. Normally to find yesterday's date, Al would move his finger to the left one space. However, since today is Sunday, it is at the start of a row. So, Al must move his finger to the end of the row above to find yesterday. Yesterday's date was Saturday, May 4.

today's date

May   yesterday

Sun	Mon	Tue	Wed	Thu	Fri	Sat
	tomorrow		1	2	3	4
(5)	6	7	8	9	10	11
12	13	14	15	16	17	18
19	20	21	22	23	24	25
26	27	28	29	30	31	

Activity Box

Fill in the blanks.

If today's date is Thursday, November 21; yesterday's date was _____.

If today's date is Tuesday, December 10; tomorrow's date will be _____.

Let's Practice!

Leti looks at her family's calendar at home. Leti's mom writes important events on the calendar.

May

Library books due

Leti - Dentist

Haru's birthday party

Max - Baseball Game

Dad's birthday

Sun	Mon	Tue	Wed	Thu	Fri	Sat
			1	2	3	4
5	6	7	8	9	10	11
12	13	14	15	16	17	18
19	20	21	22	23	24	25
26	27	28	29	30	31	

Use the calendar on page 20 to answer the questions below. Leti drew a circle around today's date.

How many days ago did Leti go to the dentist?

How many days until Leti's library books are due?

Is Leti's dad's birthday the day before or the day after Haru's birthday party?

How many more weeks until Max's baseball game?

Activity Box

Look at your calendar at home. Was your birthday before today's date or after? Count how many days, weeks, or months until your next birthday.

Glossary

calendar A tool used to measure time in days, weeks, months, and years

clock A tool used to measure time in seconds, minutes, and hours

column A line of things that runs up and down

date The number of the day in a month

day A unit of time; there are 24 hours in one day

leap year Every four years; a year when there are 366 days with February having 29 days

1 week = 7 days	1 year = 365 or 366 days
1 month = 28, 29, 30, or 31 days	1 year = 52 weeks
1 month = about 4 weeks	1 year = 12 months